Not My First Walk
on the Moon

poems by

Linda Hillman Chayes

Finishing Line Press
Georgetown, Kentucky

Not My First Walk
on the Moon

For Michael
Dan, Jess, Ben and Sarah

ACKNOWLEDGMENTS

The author gratefully acknowledges the following publications:

The RavensPerch—"Congregation" and "Necessary Crimes"
Beyond Words—"Turner's Paintings of the Sea at Margate"
2 Horatio—"When the World"
The Wild Roof—"July Again"
Quartet—"You Two"

Publisher: Leah Huete de Maines
Editor: Christen Kincaid
Cover Art and Design: Dan Chayes
Author Photo: Michael Chayes

Order online: www.finishinglinepress.com
also available on amazon.com

Author inquiries and mail orders:
Finishing Line Press
PO Box 1626
Georgetown, Kentucky 40324
USA

Contents

Turner's Paintings of the Sea at Margate
for my mother

Were you that outline in the boat falling
into the horizon—an unspecified figure

blown loose by wind and wave, open
to interpretation or storm? Churning color,

lit from inside like regret, the way you
gave up painting and everything you loved.

The horizon dissolves in the thickened
layers of strokes, a streak of black

working its way across the middle
of the canvas. Storms, as if

one could become unassailable. Or
were you one of the figures of breeze

and light, walking the piers and beaches?
Here, but going somewhere else.

Congregation

Light through large northern and southern
exposed windows make the high-ceilinged house
a chapel.

The kind of light that turns a face
into a portrait, cheeks lineated
by shadow.

As we enter the hallway midway
between windows, we shed our jackets.
No streaming sun, as the sky is lightly

overcast. No grand event as we are
here for a birthday lunch with my
step-mother, the first together in over

a year. My son says, *we'll just forget
the last year* and we begin to rewrite
history aloud leaving out the year.

*It was just last month when we met
in the city for a fish dinner and I
turned thirty.* We decide we'll drop

a year from our ages. Easily done as
one zoom-day-meal-walk merges
with hundreds. How clear and seared

our faces. Something has graced us.
There has never been a birthday before.

You Two

Before memory becomes a puzzle, I need to sift through the
momentos on my bulletin board, each photo layered.

Bored, I peel photo layered on photo until here—you
two latched to my side like lichen to a tree.

I liken a tree to a young mother in a navy polka-dotted dress.
Some islands rift from continents though they share a plate.

I should have taught you two to put your plates in the sink.
There are countless things I never expected.

One never counts on losing track of memory
or having to teach what you were never taught.

My mother taught that we are all barrier islands.
My daughter now wears my polka-dotted dress.

I wear my age like a dress that no longer fits
and stand on shifting plates that fit together like puzzles.

Still Life: Family Leaving Rockaway Beach

The setting sun frames
them

sun-dazed, shoeless,
suspended
            between here and
somewhere else.

The mother
is scraping wet sand
from her feet, grains
clinging like lint. Children
linger, their shadows
thinning spikes on the sand.

The father points out
to sea, body turned towards
another continent. One son's gaze
follows the arc
of his father's pointed reach.

The grandmother turns
to leave ahead
of the others, wrapped in shawls
from that other continent,
brim shading her face, head
bent down. So much fabric
shrouding her
            from the sun, shrouding
            stories the children

will never hear.

My grandmother Bess

lived as if the Red Army were marching down Ocean Avenue

shopped as if the banks were always failing which is to say there was
    nothing
she bought that she didn't return

kept the books and the reins on her horserace-loving husband Al

sat with the ladies on the sidewalk dropping tales of weddings and
pogroms.

Forget time-lines. History is shaped like the sweater draped over her
shoulder.

Another Fourth of July

When I fell for you, America,
I was a child catching fireflies in
glass jars as the moon rose, wanting

to own the shimmer and flash. Like
you I bungled one promise at a time
until I too tarnished my name. Now,

your name is wildfire. People are
dropping in elevators, forests, trucks, in
alleys, in deserts and parking lots.

I can't trace them as greed grenades
our hands, our brain. A man-made
draught of grief, flash flooding on

over-ridden coasts. We are both
unhoused, thin as slivers. Broken.
Heartened, in the backyard,

I toss my few remaining words
into night as my mood cycles—full,
half, crescent, crescent, half, full.

My Eustachian Tubes are Clogged

Zipped into a space suit and without
                                    sufficient gravity.
When I chew, my teeth make   .
                                    the sound of gears in my ear
Cocooned in my cold, swollen-eyed
                                    and congested, I taste jet fuel,
vibrate with the fiery jettisons of take-off.

This is not my first walk on the moon.

The summer of '69 and contorted with awe, I transmit myself right
into the small box set in my parents' bedroom, join Neil and Buzz

for lift-off, orbits, dockings
                                    and—such a near thing
with seconds left until fuel runs out
                                    Neil finally finds one spot
without crater or craggy rock and
                                    graces the touch down—

Today,

in my astronaut suit, I stoop over
                                    to gather samples of rock and moon dust.
The fine but glassy grains pop
                                    off the arid ground without help from wind.
Can you see my small steps
                                    through the moon's luminescent dustscape,
the impression of my feet
                          on the waterless Sea of Tranquility?

Necessary Crimes

1. Lessons of childhood

Like a wolf, I chose hunger
until the odds improved. I learned
to hold my words like a hand of cards;
small fingers, ravaged nails, gripping
scheming. To prevent spoilage, I swallowed
needs like mother's milk. I learned to forage
for words, sniff out smoke signals.
Biding time, timed out, losing a future.

2. Clues were everywhere

in the way the north light filtered
through Forest Hills windows
illuminating stripes on the somber
upholstery—a sepia childhood,

in two young parents asleep on the pull-
out couch, the seams splitting between them
in silence, in a baby falling from a crib
with a scar forever beneath her brow,

in the boy who comes home from school and puts
his hand through a pane of glass. Not enough
stitches to hold one family.

3. Cold Case

The case should be resolved,
boxed, shelved. Still, I stand
in each line-up, pay
everyone's penalties.
My eyes say *arrest me*.

This is me, a photograph

cracked and aging,
my father carried in his wallet
until the day he turned away.

On the beach, three-years-old,
eyes wide with desire, dark
curly hair untamable, clear
plastic inner tube hugging
my waist like a halo.

He kept the photo like a totem,
worn paper thin by too much
attention or neglect. Scalloped
edges curled behind the fogged
see-through picture holder.

One story goes I almost drowned.

One story goes my father removed the photo
from his battered thin leather wallet on the day
he left my mother.
My children will never forgive me.

I learned to tame the hair, coat
the eyes with caution, stay
afloat. No matter how many
drawers I search, there is no
photo. Yet, never more in focus.

The Facts

are never the story. Look
in one direction and the scene

falls into place like dominoes dropping in line. Step
back three feet a tree enters

the frame, its pink, peeled trunk wide
enough to hide another possible
perpetrator. Crime scene

photos fail to capture
how a face is lost
in the eyes of the other, a question

left hanging in a raised
eyebrow, the way a body sinks
into itself. Look again

and the tree is really
the lover, its shadows armed
sincere or off-the-cuff
with birds—eagles or bluejays.

Ode to my glasses

aviators, rimless, round,
neutral black plastic,
derivative blue—arriving with

the blur of the blackboard
on the brink of calculus
and first love. So many faces,

oversized professional
tortoiseshell, sly cat-eye, what
won't I let myself see…I am not

blind, but in all my dreams,
I strain to see, to raise lids
the exact weight

of an infinitesimal leaf, the
way calculus computes
instantaneous rates of change,

onto bifocals, cataracts,
buttercream fog from every
angle, sugar-high haze of aging

until surgical implants expose
every weed, wrinkle, dream. A child
again, un-, un-, I am un-glassed.

After 18 Years, She Tells the New York Times about the Rape

Like the magician I've always known I was, I
ride bareback off into the ethernet, oblivious
to wolves and tweets. The high plains are waiting.

Everyone in these parts now knows
my name. They lower their eyes as I gallop,
my invisible scars on display, wild hair flying.

In the years of nightmares, my half-mind
delivered half-lies, half-loves, binged on silence,
parsed every move, my voice too feeble to blame.

With no trees to dodge on these prairies,
I ride right past the chatter and hype, righted
by open sky, a wish for him to twist in his skin.

The wolves don't know where to go when
exposed. They hang back in their packs, hide
their teeth and appetite. Their tweets lack focus.

The roots of native grasses reach deep for water, rich
from nutrients of glacial deposits, rocks and rot. I pick up
the scent of new grass—how a life might—otherwise

Walk Along the Hudson after Lockdown

A bride and groom float Chagall-like above the walkers as
clouds disperse like nightmares evaporating.

The Hudson opens its arms, disperses its wake of applause.
A man is fishing on the wrong side of the fence.

As a man fishes under an umbrella, serenity sidles up.
Waters that are never still, the Mohicans name the river.

Two young women strike poses against a makeshift wall painted
with sunflowers, like those in Aix-en-Province where once I posed

in a bikini the color of sunflowers; providence of flesh and spirit.
Worry about nothing our bodies say when everything is ahead.

Ahead, I leap down the bank, my body turned to the river's source,
a foggy lake on the slope of Mount Marcy in the Adirondacks.

I long to hover in the fog over Lake Tear of the Clouds.
All the brides and grooms follow as the river bends.

New York Refrain, 2018

Hard to walk the sidewalks of this wrinkled
weathered city, worn to its concrete bone,
with air sticky, glimmering like mica

and yet here we are in its maze of blistering
streets, jazzy blare of horns, in the rank
subway skin-to-skin with someone's butterfly

tattoo, panning for gold in the sale racks
or stacks of the local record store, lost
in the asymmetrical designer aisles

of Bloomingdales with fluorescent lights
in our eyes, even as we have only ever
longed for the lights, the kind of exposure

where we feel both skinned to the bone
and released in all our multiplicity, relieved
of pretense, finding a refrain in weathering

dirt, fumes, fate. In this limestone
city of fossils and tempered sins, I fall
up to the water towers, turn as tough
as the tempered skin of skyscrapers.

When the world

and breath are braking,
is there any sleep to be had?

With time in play, did we speak
the day before or the day after?

When will I love air?

Isn't it enough that childhood ghosts
steal my voice?

When company arrives uninvited,
what words can be spoken?

When a word escapes me, why do all
its sidekicks knock around my brain, bickering?

Will longing, boxed, combust?
Can you reach into zoom and grab

your child from an adjacent square?

At my Desk in Front of the Dining Room Window
(January 2021)

This is me falling into my screen,
my maze, neverland, ever clicking.
It takes me everywhere, leaves me
nowhere. I lift my head.

Someone in the house across
switches on a light. I stare
at my neighbor in her window
frame, sipping tea as she loads

the laundry. She looks at me
and we are alive together as
blue winter light
ignites the bushes,

the same dim bushes that
were there yesterday and
the day before but now
the stripped forsythia

branches take the shape
of Rodin's thinker and I am in
Paris in winter, in love with
my side yard and even

my neighbor whose 70-foot
oak fell on my roof and whose
sugar-sweet indifference I
thought I would never forgive.

Claim

There is always one errant drip.
It doesn't matter how much snow we
sweep off the roof, how much sealant
we apply to seams, it persists
like the drip of intravenous fluid or a pulse
gone rogue.   A weighted blanket
—this blazing white, only securing
our chill, its brilliance flooding
the picture window so it's hard to see
where to place the pail.

                    ***

Once again, your estimate is low. An ice
damn at the eaves, warmer water
backing up behind it with nowhere to go but
through the ceiling—every snowy
year since our arrival in '91. Simply the pitch
of a roof.
            But you know the power of water to
find flow, all benign and life sustaining until
it seeps into wood, plaster and lures mold
                        and we can't breathe.

The Wind and Me

You leave the
impression on
my cheek that
I've insulted you.

In your rush from
high pressure to
low, you (sure
can) make
a person grow
small, the way
you rock
those maple
branches, your
subwoofer sound,
a kind of lullaby,
but not
the soothing kind,
more bough
breaking and
cradle falling.

In my rush
between highs
and lows, I
wish I had
your energy,
your firm
push, breath
of a gale.

Lemon Spring

Now, upright and urgent stalks
of mature, broad forsythia
fill what was once air, claim
the space around them

By the proud forsythia shrubs that line
the edge, their screening now about complete,
here, weeks ago thin sticks wavered
in the wind like my changing moods, miniature
leaves in timid greens, young, in anxious play.

Overnight they were alive in showy yellow,
bellowing like a teen Look at me. I watched
through the window, surprised again,
as if I had never suspected a lemon spring.

Blueberries

Black-blue buddies
bunched like best friends
explode the cereal bowl
with their generosity.

Blue blue berries flaunt
their sweet, breathe
their ripe into my stride,
raise velocity, block

a howl rising
at the back of my throat
as if they knew
the enormity.

No worries, at lunch
they convene again
as best friends can and
make the yogurt hum,

lure my blues right
into an indigo hymn.

July Again

Something is askew this summer.
By that I mean it has rained so
often that the garden is bloated,
hydrangeas unfolding into azaleas
astilbe tangling with epimedium,
wild stalks weaving one
single covering of shrub

and then the white butterflies
in pairs,
spinning so close
to each other
you'd have to assume
invisible strings.
Synchronized swimmers,
their dance
choreographed by pheromones
or passion.

They touch down
tickling the angelonia, so
brief and tender
the swollen garden hardly
notices.

Almost unreal, a moon-white butterfly,
but there are so many.

I am full with them,
their kisses, their
philandering flights.

Linda Hillman Chayes is a poet and psychoanalyst. Her work explores the ongoing process of knowing who we are in the context of our family's stories (past and present) as well as our social and cultural environment. Her previous chapbook, *The Lapse* was published by Finishing Line Press in 2014, and her poems have appeared or are forthcoming in *Kestrel, The American Poetry Journal, Quartet, The Westchester Review, 2 Horatio, The RavensPerch, The Wild Roof, Beyond Words*, and other publications. She practices as a psychologist/psychoanalyst in New York City and Westchester County. She co-wrote and co-edited a book *The Voice of the Analyst: Narratives in Developing a Psychoanalytic Identity* published by Routledge Press in 2018.